William in the Snow

'Get up William!' shouted Julie. 'Lo[...]
window and you'll get a surprise.'

William got out of bed and pulled back the
curtains. There were icy patterns all over the
glass. They looked like ferns or feathers. William
breathed on the glass and rubbed a little hole
in the ice with his finger so he could see out.
'Snow!' he gasped. 'Great! It looks really deep!'

He got dressed as fast as he could and ran
downstairs. Mum was out so William's big sister had
been left in charge.

'You're not going out without your breakfast,' said
Julie, 'and you're not going out dressed like that.
Put your football socks and wellingtons on and go
and find your gloves and scarf.'

'I won't be cold. I'll be running about,' said
William.

'You won't be cold because you'll be wearing what
I've told you to wear,' replied Julie.

'I know you want to be a teacher when you grow
up,' said William, 'but why must you practise on me?'

2

While William was having his breakfast Hamid came round. 'Hurry up,' said Hamid. 'I've brought my old sledge. I thought we could go to Waterlowe Park.'

'Great idea!' said William.

Hamid's sledge was an old-fashioned one. It was made of wood and had steel runners but it was much faster and stronger than a modern plastic sledge. It was big and strong enough to carry William and Hamid at the same time, so that added to the fun.

The boys pulled the sledge to Waterlowe Park. Most of their school friends were there already. There were long steep slopes in the park and the snow was perfect for sledging.

At the bottom of one of the slopes was the lake. The water had frozen and there were notices telling people to keep off the thin ice. 'Look at the poor ducks,' said Hamid. 'They've got no water to swim in. They look fed up.'

'There are no quacks in the ice,' laughed William.

Sledging was great fun. It took ages to pull the sledge to the top of the slope but it was worth it. Hamid and William usually fell off long before the sledge reached the bottom of the slope. But that was part of the fun too. 'What do you hear if you send a snowman into a haunted house?' asked William.

'I give up,' said Hamid.

'Iced screams,' laughed William.

Everybody was having a wonderful time. But suddenly things changed. A snowball hit Hamid on the ear. It was a really hard snowball and Hamid began to cry. 'Oh no,' said William. 'It's Toby Keene and Jim Bowman!' Toby and Jim were roaring with laughter.

'Earwig-o! Earwig-o! Earwig-o!' shouted Toby. The two bullies ran up to William and Hamid. 'May we borrow your sledge, please?' grinned Jim.

'No!' said Hamid.

'Thank you ever so much,' said Toby, snatching it.

Toby and Jim got on the sledge and shot down the slope. They crashed into some other sledges on the way, and they thought this was terrific fun.

'What can we do?' asked Hamid.

'We'll just have to wait until they get tired of it,' said William. 'We can't do anything else.'

But Toby and Jim were enjoying themselves. It began to look as if they were never going to give the sledge back to Hamid.

After a long time Toby shouted up the slope. 'We're off now,' he called. 'If you want your rotten old sledge you'll have to come and get it.'

'Oh no!' said Hamid. They're going towards the lake.' He ran down the slope and William ran after him. 'Hamid!' shouted William. 'Don't go near the lake. You don't know what they might do.'

Toby stood on the frozen lake holding the sledge. Even Jim Bowman looked worried. 'Don't be an idiot, Toby!' he said. 'Can't you read the notices?'

But Toby didn't listen. He pulled the sledge further away from the edge of the lake. 'If you want your sledge you'll have to come and get it,' he laughed.

'Come back,' shouted William. 'You'll fall in!'

'Give me my sledge!' shouted Hamid.

'Come and get it!' sneered Toby, and he began to jump up and down on the ice. 'It's quite safe,' he called. 'These notices are just here to scare people. It's great for sliding. Come on, Jim! It's fantast . . .'

There was a loud cracking sound as Toby fell
through the ice. 'Oh no!' yelled Jim.

'What an idiot!' said William.

'My sledge!' wailed Hamid.

'Help! Mummy!' yelled Toby.

Toby was up to his chest in the freezing water. He
couldn't climb out because the ice was too slippery.

'What are we going to do?' gasped Jim.

'You go and get the Park Keeper. We'll stay here
and try to think of something,' said William.

By the side of the lake was an old tree. The weight of the snow had broken off one of its branches. 'We can't go on the ice,' said William, 'but we might be able to pull him out with that branch.'

'Hurry up,' yelled Toby, 'I'm turning into a block of ice.'

The branch was very heavy but the two boys managed to drag it to the edge of the lake and push it out to Toby. It seemed to take ages but, at last, Toby was able to grab hold of it.

William and Hamid pulled and pulled but they were
not strong enough to pull Toby out of the hole in
the ice. 'I want to go home!' he cried.

At last Jim ran up with the Park Keeper. She had
a long pole and she was able to reach Toby with it.
They all helped pull him out. 'You silly little
boy,' she snapped. 'Can't you read the notices? You
might have drowned.' Then she made him take off his
wet things and wrap himself in the blankets she and
Jim had brought.

12

She used the pole to pull Hamid's sledge to the edge
of the lake. 'Go right away from here,' she said
to William and Hamid. 'You two troublemakers can
come with me.'

'He didn't even say thank you,' said Hamid when
Toby and Jim had gone.

'Never mind,' said William, 'he won't bother us
again. And he certainly did the ducks a favour.'
Hamid looked at the ducks swimming happily in the
hole that Toby had made. 'They must have thought
Toby was quackers!' he laughed.

All About Snow and Ice

I bet you know what water looks like. You'll have watched it come out of the tap. You may have seen it in rivers, lakes, and the sea. Then there's frozen water which we call ice, and the tiny droplets of very hot water we call steam. But some water you can't have seen. When water is heated by the sun, it turns into a gas called water vapour.

You can't see water vapour even though it is all around you, in the air. When it is very cold, water vapour freezes and turns into tiny ice crystals. No two ice crystals have the same shape though each one has six sides. When a number of ice crystals stick together a snowflake is formed.

Ice is frozen water. If raindrops freeze they fall as hailstones. When a pond freezes it is covered in a layer of ice. It's not safe to walk on a frozen pond as it's difficult to tell how thick the ice is.

There are good points and bad points about snow and ice. Here are some of the bad points. Roads become slippery and dangerous. Towns and villages can be cut off by snowdrifts. Farm animals can be trapped under layers of snow. Branches and whole trees can be toppled over by the weight of snow. Water pipes can freeze and burst. People can slip on icy pavements and be injured. Can you think of any more? What are the good points about snow and ice?

The Bear's Tail

One cold winter's day a polar bear was walking
across the ice, looking for something to eat, when
he met a fox. The fox was looking very pleased with
himself because he had just stolen ten fat fish
from a hunter's storehouse.

'Will you give me some of those fish, please?'
asked the bear. 'I'm very hungry and I can't find
anything to eat.'

'I'm afraid I need these fish for my family,'
replied the fox, 'but there are plenty more where
they came from.'

16

'Where did you get them?' asked the bear.

'I fished for them,' replied the fox.

'But I don't have a fishing line,' said the bear sadly.

'You don't need one,' laughed the fox. 'All you do is find a place where the ice is thin and make a hole in it. Under the ice is the sea. Then you dip your tail into the water and wait for the fish to come and nibble at it. After about an hour you pull your tail out of the hole and you will find ten, twenty, perhaps thirty fish hanging on to it.'

'Is that supposed to be a joke?' frowned the bear. 'I'm not stupid you know. Nobody could catch thirty fish in an hour.'

'You'll see,' smiled the fox. 'I caught ten in a few minutes and my tail isn't as long as yours.'

The bear thanked the fox for his help, made a hole in the ice, and dipped his magnificent white tail down into the sea.

The water was freezing and very soon the bear's tail began to sting. 'Oh good,' thought the bear. 'The fish are starting to nibble. Only another fifty-five minutes to go!'

In the village where the humans lived, a hunter
found that his fish had been stolen. He snatched
up his spear and set out to follow the fox's
footprints through the snow.
After a while the fox's footprints became mixed up
with the footprints of the huge bear. 'That's lucky,'
smiled the hunter. 'A warm bearskin is just what I
need.' He forgot about the stolen fish and the fox
and started to track the bear.

By now the bear's tail had frozen into the ice.
When he tried to pull it out of the hole to see how
many fish he had caught, he couldn't move. 'Oh no!'
he gasped. 'That naughty fox has made a fool of me.'
He pulled and he tugged but he couldn't escape. It
was then that he saw the hunter running towards him
across the ice. With a howl of rage the bear gave a
tremendous jump and, leaving behind his beautiful
white tail, he made his escape. Ever since that day
bears have had short stumpy tails.

Why the Bear Sleeps Through the Winter

In Lapland where the reindeer live and the winter nights are long and cold, the people tell this story.

Once, long ago, on the first warm day of spring, an old man was walking through the melting snow. He walked and walked until he came to a mighty river that rushed and roared along its rocky bed. The river was so swollen with melted snow and ice that it had flooded the fields and washed away the little wooden bridge over which the old man had hoped to cross.

The old man stood and looked at the icy water and scratched his head, and wondered, and wondered what he was going to do.

On the far bank of the river stood a horse, nipping and pulling at the few blades of fresh green grass that had pushed themselves up through the snow. 'I'm sorry to trouble you,' shouted the old man, 'but I'd be very glad if you would help me. Would you carry me across this river on your back? It's too deep for me to wade across, but you could manage it quite easily.'

'Can't you see that I'm busy eating?' snapped the
horse unkindly. 'I've not had a good feed all
winter. Now that this juicy green grass has started to
grow I'm going to eat as much of it as I can.'

'It would only take you a moment,' pleaded the
old man.

'Go away and leave me in peace,' said the horse,
and he turned his back on the man and continued to
nibble at the grass.

The old man walked down the river bank, hoping
to find another bridge or a shallow place to cross,
but he had no luck.

When he had been walking for a long time he saw
a reindeer on the far bank running and jumping in
the spring sunshine. 'Well, he looks strong and
lively,' thought the old man. 'I'm sure he'll
agree to carry me across the river.' He called to
the reindeer and begged a ride on his back.

'Certainly not!' laughed the reindeer. 'All
through the winter I've had to pull sledges full
of logs for my master's fire. Today it's spring
and I'm going to leap, and run and jump and
enjoy myself. Why don't you wade across?'

'But the river is too deep for me to cross on
my own,' shouted the old man.

'Hard luck!' laughed the unkind reindeer, and he
bounded off across the snowy fields.

'Oh dear,' thought the old man. 'I must reach the other side. I will just have to try and wade across.' He took two steps into the freezing water and the strong current began to knock him off balance. He was about to take a third step when a voice behind him cried, 'Stop!'

A big brown bear had been watching him all the time. It lumbered slowly towards the old man and spoke to him. 'Whatever do you think you're doing?' asked the bear. 'That river is far too deep and wide for you to cross. If you take another step you'll be swept away by the current. Don't you know how dangerous it is?'

'But what can I do?' cried the old man. 'The bridge is down. The horse and the reindeer could easily have carried me but they refused. I must get across before nightfall.'

The bear looked worried. He thought for a moment and said, 'I'll carry you on my back. It won't be easy for me because I'm very weak. Winter is a hard, miserable time for bears. We find very little food to eat in the forest, and the snow and ice makes us cold and tired. But at least I have a much better chance of crossing the river than you do, so climb on my back.'

The old man thanked the bear and climbed on his
back. The two of them waded slowly into the fast-
flowing waters. The bear shuddered and stumbled
as the current caught him. Branches and broken logs
banged against his sides and he began to think that
they would never reach the other side. As he waded
deeper the stones on the river bed slipped from
under his paws and many times he was almost swept
away by the flood. 'If I'm bowled over,' he
thought, 'we shall both be swept over the waterfall
at the bottom of the valley.' But he kept these
thoughts to himself as he didn't want to scare the
old man who was clinging nervously on to his back.

At last the river grew shallow again and although
he was almost frozen to death and exhausted, the
bear knew that they would be safe. He managed
to scramble up the bank, and collapsed in a cold wet
heap. The old man jumped from his back and danced
with joy. 'Thank you, bear!' he cried, 'Thank you.'

'Don't mention it,' gasped the bear. 'I was happy
to be of use.' But when he looked at the old man
he saw that something strange was happening to him.
The weak old man was changing into a powerful young
man.

When he spoke, his squeaky old man's voice had grown deep and powerful. 'I am the god, Ukku,' said the young man. 'The horse and the reindeer would not help me and, because they refused, they shall be hungry and hard-working in the cold days of winter until the end of time. But you, Bear, because you showed me kindness, you shall eat and grow fat in the warm days of autumn. All through the terrible months of winter I will wrap you in a warm, deep sleep. You will dream of sweet nuts, juicy berries and sticky honey, and you won't wake up until the warm days of spring return.'

So now you know, if you can believe such things, why bears sleep through the cold winter months.

How the Chipmunk Got His Stripes

This small animal is a chipmunk. Can you see the
broad stripes down his back? In Russia they tell
a story to explain how the stripes got there.

A bear once woke up after a long winter sleep.
He had eaten nothing since the autumn and was very
hungry so he set off to find something to eat.
He searched all day but there was no food to be
found. Just as he was beginning to give up hope, he
came across an old tree stump in the forest. 'There
might be some honey in this stump,' he thought and
he began to dig it up with his long, sharp claws.

Suddenly a chipmunk popped his head out of a hole
in the tree stump. 'Hey! What do you think you're
doing? I live here!'

'Oh dear!' gasped the bear. 'I'm very sorry. I
was looking for something to eat. I thought there
might be some honey in this old stump.'

'Old stump! Old stump!' snapped the chipmunk. 'It
may be an old stump to you, but it's my home! If you
want something to eat, wait there and I'll go and
find you something. What sort of animal is it
that doesn't have a snack ready for when he wakes
up? I don't know what the world's coming to!'

When the chipmunk returned he was no longer in a
bad temper. He gave the bear a big pile of nuts
and roots that he had fetched from his autumn
store. 'Help yourself,' smiled the chipmunk. 'I've
got plenty more.'

The bear ate a good meal and growled contentedly.
'You're only a little animal,' he laughed, 'but
you're a good and kind one.' And he gently stroked
the chipmunk's back with his great big paw. The
bear's claws left dark stripes in the chipmunk's
fur, and that is why, even to this day, the
chipmunk has a striped coat.